# Swing Trading

### *How to Make Money*
### *in Less Than 7 Days*

**Charles Reis**

# Table of Contents

# Introduction

Congratulations on purchasing this book and thank you for doing so.

The following chapters will discuss everything that you need to know to get started with swing trading. Swing trading uses a lot of the same strategies and methods that are needed with day trading, but you are allowed to do a trade between one day and two weeks, rather than just getting a few hours to complete the trade. This takes away some of the stress and makes it easier for you to work in the stock market, but you will love all the profit that you can make in a short amount of time.

We will discuss what swing trading all about, some of the benefits that come with swing is trading, as well as some of the strategies that you can use to be successful when you enter into a trade. We will also discuss some of the rules that you have to follow with swing trading and how to avoid some of the common beginner mistakes that can help you earn a lot of money.

Swing trading can be a great way to earn a big profit in a short amount of time to the stock market. Start learning more about swing trading with this guidebook that's designed to give you an easy read with concise information.

There are plenty of books on this subject on the market, thanks again for choosing this one! Every effort was made to ensure it is full of as much useful information as possible, please enjoy!

# Chapter 1:

# What is Swing Trading?

Picking out a good type of investment can be hard. You want to pick out one that will bring you a good amount of profit in the process, but you also need to limit your risk, or you could lose out on everything in the long run. You have a variety of options when it comes to trading. You can choose to invest in the stock market over the long term or with day trading. You can start your own business and let this be your investment. And you can also work in real estate or other similar investments.

If you want to have the potential to earn a lot of money with investing in a short amount of time, then you may want to consider working with swing trading. Swing trading tries to capture the gains as possible with any stock, or financial instrument, within an overnight hold over for several weeks. This is a short-term investment which means you will not hold onto your position for many years, but it gives you a little more time than you would have with day trading and some other investment options. The traders who work in swing trading may use either the intrinsic or the fundamental value of a stock while also taking a look at the patterns and price trends that come with the stock to help them make some good decisions.

So, how does swing trading work compared to some of the other investment opportunities? To start, all traders need to act quickly to find situations where a particular stock has a big potential to move upwards in a short amount of time. This needs to be some unusual upward trend that is about to happen, something that others may miss out on but a trader will recognize when looking at the trends, the news, and other information.

If you can trade on these trends, purchasing the stock when it is at a lower price, holding onto it for up to a few weeks, and then selling when that huge upward trend ends up happening.

For the most part, swing trading is something that occurs with day traders, especially individuals and those that work at home in this market. Most large institutions will be too big and have too many assets to move out of the stocks quickly enough to make this worth their time. This is one of the benefits of being an individual trader; you can move around the market much faster than big companies can, allowing you to earn a lot of profit in the process.

A swing trader is either going to hold a short or a long position, and they need to hold this position for one night up to a few weeks. The goal here is to get a larger amount of profit than you could with day trading by hoping the market moves up even more. With swing trading, you will assume that a larger price move and range will occur, which means that you need to pick your position carefully to minimize your risks. And when you work with time frame charts, you would rely on some that are a bit larger, such as hour, daily, and weekly charts based on what you think the market will do.

## How is swing trading different from day trading?

The first question that you may have is how swing trading and day trading are different from each other. They both try and go after some of the trends that are going on in the market, and they are both short-term trades that you can work with.

The biggest difference that you will find with day trading and swing trading is how long you will hold your position. With day trading, you will purchase and sell the stock all on the same day before the market closes. With swing trading, you need to hold onto the stock at least overnight, if not up to a few weeks, depending on how the trend is going and how much you would like to make.

This can add in a little more risk and unpredictability to your trade. It is hard to know what gaps or up and down movements will happen in your position overnight, which is why most swing traders will be done using smaller position sizes than they would with day trading.

You get some choice in how long you would like to hold onto your position, which can reduce the risk a little bit. But it is always a good idea to have an idea of how long you will stay in the market ahead of joining. So, before you decide to go with a swing trade, you will sit and look over the charts, decide how long it will be until the upward trend occurs, and then stick with that as part of your plan. Yes, the market may keep going up, but having this in place ahead of time will ensure that you can keep the emotions out of the game and will give you the biggest profit with the smallest amount of risk as possible.

As a swing trader, you will be responsible for looking at chart patterns over many days. Some of the most common patterns that you will find include triangles, flags, head and shoulders patterns, cup and handle patterns, and even moving average crossovers. You can also find reversal candlesticks, like hammers and shooting stars will help you to figure out the best time to join the market and make the biggest profit possible.

Swing trading has more risk than some of the longer -term options that you may choose to go with. With the long-term investments, you will find that you have the time and the relaxation to not worry about the big ups and downs in the market as much. Your account will end up evening out if you stay on the market long enough.

But with swing trading, this is not always going to work. You are only going to be in the market for up to a few weeks at the most. This means that if a trend does not go your way, you will lose out on money. You must do your research diligently before starting and make sure that you can accurately read the market. You only get a few weeks, which is more than what a day trader will get to work with, but adds in more risk, especially when you are working in an overnight position.

You have the choice of many investments, but if you would like to earn a lot of money within a week or less, then swing trading may be the option that you are looking for. Let's take a look at some of the strategies that you can use when it comes to swinging trading to ensure you are getting the best results possible.

## The mindset of a swing trader

The mindset of someone who wants to work as a swing trader will be a bit different than you would find with some of the other trading styles that are out there. Many investments are long term. You may get into the stock market and hope to make a good profit over a couple of years, or you will set it up for your retirement plan. You can go with real estate and do rentals or sell over a few years as well. Even starting a business is something you will work on for the majority of your life rather than just a few weeks or months.

With swing trading, you will do all of your investing within a few weeks. Yes, you can continue to do this for the long term and do it for many years, but each trade will take no longer than a few weeks. If your trades end up taking longer than this time limit, then you are getting out of swing trading and your strategy is not really going to work. Because of the differences between short term and long term investing, it takes a special kind of trader to get into swing trading and see a good amount of success.

So, what does a swing trader need to have, what kind of personality, to be successful? First, they need to be able to think things through without emotions. Things can change quickly when you are a day trader, and your money can often be at risk. Since you are not working with the investment for the long-term, it is possible to lose that money quickly without a chance to gain it back. This can be hard on a lot of new investors and can often negatively influence the trades that they make.

If you are someone who has trouble with their emotions and who likes to get caught up at the moment, then swing trading is not the right option for you. On the other hand, if you can make rational decisions from the start and stick with them, swing trading can be a great way to make a lot of money in a short amount of time.

Next on the list is a love of research and charts. You have to be able to spend time looking at lots of charts and decide when a new trend is coming up for one of the stocks that you want to work with. Each stock that you work with will have a number of charts to look over, and this can give you an idea of the trends that have gone on with that particular stock, something that is very useful in swing trading. You also need to be able to look at the charts for the market as a whole. Many times a stock will go with the market, or at least will be influenced by how the market is behaving. It is never a good idea to jump into a swing trade without looking at not only the charts for the stock you are interested in but also looking at the charts on the market as a whole.

Another thing that many swing traders need to be able to do is to predict when a trend will happen. You want to find a stock that is undervalued right now, one that is not being bought all that much and is being sold at a lower price. The trick though is that you need to look at the charts and see that a big upward trend is about to happen. If you can purchase that stock at the lower price and wait out a few days for that trend to happen, you can make a big profit once it occurs. This is the biggest advantage to swing trading, but if you are not able to find the trends ahead of time, you will miss out.

Swing trading is a bit different than some of the other trading options that you may choose to go with. It is fast-paced, can bring in a lot of emotions along the way, and has the potential for a lot of profits if you learn how to do it the right way. But when you learn the different strategies and have a lot of the mindset requirements above, you can see a lot of success when it comes to swing trading.

# Chapter 2:

# The Benefits of Swing Trading

With all of the different types of investing that you can choose to go with, you may be wondering why you should decide to go with swing trading. Long-term investments often have a lower risk, but they don't earn money very quickly. Real estate can help you to be hands on, but then you need to deal with your tenants and other people who can be a hassle. Each type of investment will provide you with some rewards and some risks, so what is so enticing about swing trading?

There are actually quite a few benefits that you will get when it comes to swing trading. Some of the biggest benefits that a lot of traders enjoy include:

- **Swing trading has less risk:** When compared to working with day trading, you will find that swing trading has less risk. This is because you get more time to work in the market. It is often hard to estimate how a stock will do throughout a single day. But it is easier to predict whether a stock will do better over a few days if there is a trend for this or there is a big news event that will change the market. This lower risk helps make swing trading more profitable and appealing to many traders.

- **You can swing trade along with other trades:** Many traders will choose to work on swing trading along with day trading all at the same time. During the market hours, they will focus most of their energy on their day trading position. To make this happen you will need to make sure that you place the swing trades the night before, or during premarket, so that you don't get distracted by the wrong things when it is time to trade.

- **Overnight trading can be an advantage:** Some traders believe that trading overnight will harm them. They are worried about some of the trends that could happen to their stock while they are asleep. But for others, these overnight positions can help them to earn more money. Some gaps will occur overnight that will go in the direction that your trade wants. If the overnight position works the way that you would like, it means that you can make a lot of money overnight, something that is not available with day trading or some of the other trading strategies.

- **More time to look at the market:** day trading has to be done really quickly. You don't get a lot of time to watch the markets, and you may need to make split-second decisions to get results. With swing trading, you can analyze the market over time, and you have more time to make your trading decisions. This takes away some of the pressure of your trades, and it is easier to earn money in this manner without all the stress.

- **Potential to reach the trades better:** Compared to working with day trading, you are more likely to reach the trades that you would like with swing trading. You will be able to watch the market, predict how the trades will do over a few days or a few weeks, rather than a few hours, and make more money. There is potential to make a lot of money overnight with this trading style, but you can also hold your position longer if the upward trend doesn't occur at the right time.

- **More daily freedom:** If you are a day trader, you have to spend all day watching your trades. Little changes up or down in the market will make a big difference in day trading, and this can be really stressful if you are getting started. Many of the people who decide to go with swing trading tried out day trading in the past but didn't like all the stress that went with it and didn't like having to stare at their computer screens all day long. Swing trading can provide you with a similar profit without all the hassle.

Swing trading and day trading may have some parts that are similar, but some big differences can make swing trading a more viable option for many traders.

# Chapter 3:

# How to Get Started Swing Trading

Now that you know a little bit more about swing trading, it is time to get into the market and start making some money along the way. It isn't enough for you to just hear about swing trading and then stare at the stock market. Instead, you need to be able to pick out your strategy, work with a good broker, and get into the market as quickly as possible.

The first thing that you need to do is pick out a good broker to work with. These brokers can make a big difference in how well your trades will go overall. They can place the trades for you, will offer you some advice when it is needed, and so much more. There are a variety of different types of brokers you can work with, and it often depends on the features that you would like, how much you want to spend, and how much help you will need in the process. Do some research on the best brokers in your area to help you see the best results.

You also need to figure out which analysis tools you would like to use. You need to have a few in place because this helps you to understand which trend is coming up better than just relying on one at a time. We will take a look at some of the tools that you can use for swing trading and the strategies so that you can pick the one that is the best for you.

Once you pick out the analysis tool you want to use, you need to spend some time researching it and learning exactly how they work. Your broker will be able to provide you with a few of these tools, so that can make things easier, but you should also look at some of your own. The more research you can do before entering the trade, the better chance you will have with catching the trend and making the biggest amount of profit.

Next, you need to take some time and pick out which strategy you would like to use. Several strategies work well, but you need to be able to go with one strategy and stick with it the whole time. Each strategy is different and will require you to enter the market in a different way, which is why you need to stick with one strategy and learn how to use it correctly.

Choosing a good strategy is probably going to be one of the hardest things to do. They all work differently and will require you to look at the charts in a different way than the others. And if you mess up with a strategy or you try to mix them up in the middle of a trade, you will end up losing a lot of money in the process. This can be stressful for someone who is new to the swing trading business. Make sure you fully learn how each strategy is supposed to work and even discuss some of them with your broker ahead of time to help you pick the right one.

You also need to take the time to get started with your trades. Your broker will be able to help you out with this part. Either they can give you advice on the trades that you will work with or you can tell them the rules that you want to follow. Either way, it is best for them to put the trades in for you since they can get the work done quickly.

When placing your trades, make sure that you place your stop points. You need a stop point for losing and earning money. These are points where you will exit the market and can reduce your risk. If the market ends up going down to your stop loss point, it means it is time to get out of the market. Some beginners may want to sit around and wait to see if their losses will reverse, but this allows the emotions to get into the mix and can result in a big loss of money. Once your market reaches your preset stop loss point, it is time to exit the market and cut your losses.

You need a stop point on the other side of things as well. This helps you to get your profits and know when you should leave the market, even if the market goes back up. Since you are trading over a short amount of time, you want to ensure that you will reach your profits without losing money if things reverse. Putting this stop point in place will help you to make as much profit as possible while reducing your risk as well.

When the trade has been successful, you can be done with your first round of swing trading. Some of the trades will happen overnight, and others will take a few weeks to accomplish, but most of the time you will complete your trade and earn your profit in a relatively short time period. You can then take your profit and move on to your next trade.

## Tips for swing trading

Getting started with swing trading is a great option. It can help you to make a lot of money in a short amount of time, but there is a level of risk that you will need to deal with. Understanding how to get into the market, how to read the charts, and so on will help you to get the results that you would like. When you are ready to get started with swing trading, make sure to follow some of these great tips:

- **Pick a strategy that is easy:** Some beginners think that complex strategies are the best to increase their profits. But these complex strategies can be really confusing and overwhelming for someone who is just beginning. Go with a simple strategy, at least until you learn more about the market.

- **Start in one place:** Many beginner traders will start out by trying out too many markets at once. This can make it hard to know what you are doing. Stick with one market and one pattern and concentrate on that for now.

- **Don't forget a stop loss:** This is one of the main reasons that a trader will lose all their money. They will forget the stop loss and not watch the market enough, resulting in a huge loss in the process. Always use stop orders to help you reduce your risk.

- **Trade in both directions:** The best way to make money in swing trading is to trade on both sides of the market. If you spend your whole time trading on the long side, you will miss half of your trading opportunities.

- **Keep a good risk to reward ratio:** This ratio needs to be at least one to three. Remember that you are trading short term so you will not make a ton of money in the process. You can make a decent profit, but you won't make many thousands over this time. Ensure that you stay with a good risk to reward ratio so that you will make some money without losing everything.

- **Don't trade inside a vacuum:** One issue that a beginner will face is that they will only take a look at a chart or two and then they forget what is going on elsewhere. You need to look through the news to see what information will change the value of a stock. You need to look at various charts. You basically need to get your information from as many places as possible to help you get the best results.

- **Look at market indicators:** These market indicators can help you to determine which way your trading will go and are not things that you should avoid looking through.

- **Go with the trend:** Another mistake that some beginners will make is that they will not look at some of the long-term analysis tools that can help them to see which direction the market will take. While these focus more on the long-term, they can help you with some of your short-term trades as well.

- **Don't impose your will on your market:** You will not have any ability to control the market at all. If the market starts to move away from what you want, you will not win just by telling it to change. Your job is to figure out where the market is going and then try to keep your trades going with the market. You need to learn the market and how it works; you can't expect the market to work the way that you would like.

Working with swing trading can be a great way to make a lot of money in a short amount of time. It is not always the easiest and can cause some more risk compared to some of the other trading methods that you may try. But the more you learn how to read the charts and follow the market, and the more experience you get out of swing trading, the more money you will be able to make.

# Chapter 4:

# Top Strategies for

# Success with Swing Trading

To see success with swing trading, you need to make sure that you are working on the right strategy. There are a lot of different strategies that you can work with when you are ready to join the market, and each of them has potential to earn you a profit if you properly use them. But you have to know how each of them will work and you need to stick with that strategy throughout your whole time trading.

This chapter will talk about how to trade in swing trading and the different strategies that you can use. Take a look at a few of them and see which one will work the best for your trading personality.

## Looking at good patterns

One thing that you can look at is the charts for a particular stock you would like to look through. There are a lot of different patterns that can come up all the time and the way that they look will determine whether they are a good one to use for your trade or if you should go with another option. When you notice these patterns, you will be better able to predict how the stocks that you want to work with will behave in the future and use this to make a profit. Let's take a look at some of the successful swing trading patterns that you should look for when you get started.

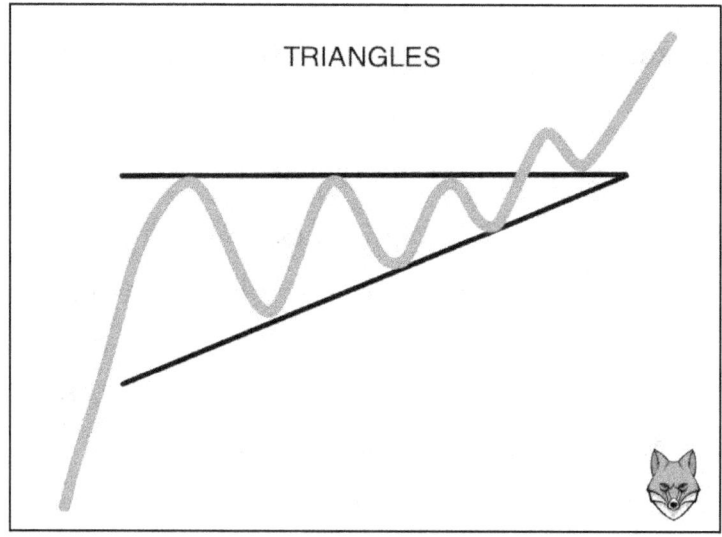

TRIANGLES

**Triangle:** The triangle shape is a very successful pattern to look for, and if you see it in one of your stocks, you will be likely to see successful. With the triangle pattern, you will notice that the trend is going either upwards or downwards, but the variations are getting smaller between the highs and the lows. When these start to get together on the right side of the triangle, you can see that a breakthrough trend is about to happen. This can go the opposite way as well. If you see a triangle that goes in the opposite way of the picture above, it means that the trend is about to go down and you should not join in.

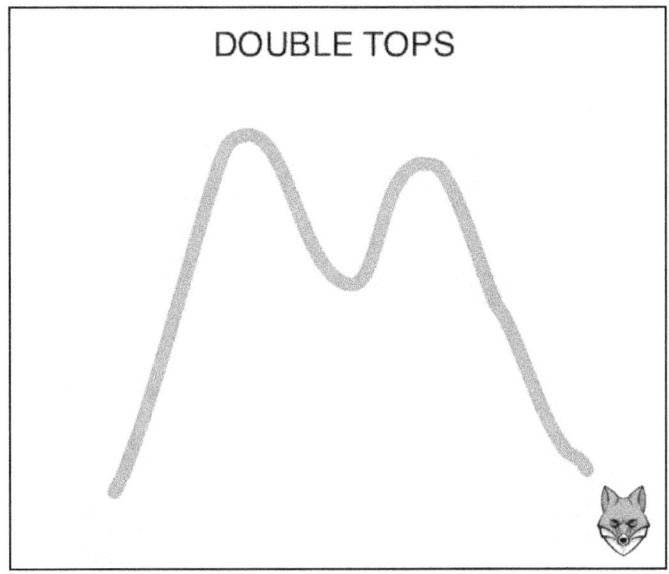

**Double Top:** this is another pattern that many swing traders will take a look at, and it can be really successful. This pattern is one that you want to look for when it comes to working with swing trading. The same pattern works even if it is turned around. For example, if you notice that this trend is upside down, you can use this information to help with going long in your stock.

**Channel Pattern:** Next on the list is the channel pattern. This is a great pattern even though it is not always as successful as some of the others. You will find this one repeating through various instruments that you may be moving. There are two ways that you can trade for this pattern. One is on the channel, and the other is to trade when there is a breakout. It often depends on which way you would like to trade with your swing trade and how the market is doing.

## The Moving Average

Another option to use is the moving average. Since swing trading can do really well with technical analysis and the moving average is considered one of these, it is a good option to go with. The two options that you can use include the exponential moving average and the simple moving average. With the simple moving average, we will look at the average of security over a specified number of time periods, such as over fifteen minutes or another time frame. The exponential moving average will spend more time looking at recent prices. The point of both of these is to identify the direction of the trend and figure out where the resistance and support levels are to make the most money possible.

One thing to notice is that these moving averages will lag from the current prices because they base themselves on the prices that happened in the past. The longer the time period you use for a moving average, the bigger lag you will deal with. This means that a 200-day MA will have a bigger lag compared to a 20-day MA because of how long of a time period it covers.

The best bet is to use shorter moving averages since you are working with a short-term trading strategy. If you decide to do a longer-term investment, you can go with a longer moving average if you would like. Often going with something near the 50-day MA is a good option because it gives you a good amount of average to work with and when breaks happen, either below or above this moving average, it can be an important signal for your trading.

You will find that moving averages are also important trading signals all on their own, but they can be important when there are two averages that will cross over. When there is a moving average that rises, it shows that the stock is going through an uptrend, but when the moving average is starting to decline, it means that the stock is starting to go on a downtrend.

In a similar manner, an upward momentum can be confirmed when you see a bullish crossover, which is something that happens when the short-term moving average starts to cross higher than the moving average for the long-term. The opposite will be true when you are looking at downward momentum with a bearish crossover.

## Candlestick charts

These are great technical tools that can hold a lot of data about the stock into one price bar. This can make them easier to look at and more useful than the traditional simple lines that will often connect the closing prices. These candlesticks will build up patterns that can predict the direction of the price once you are done with it, and the brighter colors make them easier to read through.

There are a few different types of candlestick patterns that you can work with, and each one will help you in different types of markets. You also need to find your own candlestick patterns. If you follow the ones that are given out by hedge funds and other big companies, you are being led in the wrong direction, and you won't see the results that you want. However, there are always candlestick patterns that you can follow to help you get the best results.

Here, we will look at the top candlestick patterns that you can use to help you get started no matter which market you are working in. The best ones to use to help you make a profit in swing trading includes:

**Three line strike:** The bullish three line strike reversal pattern will show you three black candles that are going down for the trend. Each of the bar posts a lower low, and then they will close near the intrabar low. Then there is a fourth bar that will open up even lower, but it reverses out into a wide-range outside the bar that closes out above the high of the first candle that was in the series. You will see that the opening print will also mark the low on your fourth bar. This kind of reversal often will predict a higher price in more than 80 percent of the trades that you can do using it.

You can also work with the two black gapping candlesticks. This is a bearish pattern that will occur after the stock has gone through a big top in an uptrend and there will be a gap down that will yield out two black bars that post lower lows. With this kind of pattern, it will predict that the stock will continue to decline even more and that there may be a more regular downtrend in the market. If you see this kind of trend, there is a higher chance that the stock will experience lower prices in the near future.

Another strategy to work with is the three black crows. This one will start at or near the high of your uptrend, and there will be three black bars that will post lower lows. This is another predictor that a decline will continue in the stock and that this trend may continue for the foreseeable future. The version that is the most bearish will start at a new high point because it will end up trapping some buyers who are entering in on momentum plays. This pattern though is often going to predict that the stock will continue with the lower prices rather than going back up.

The evening star is the next candlestick option that you can use as a strategy. This is a bearish strategy that will start with a tall white bar that carries an uptrend so that the stock ends up with a new high. The market will then gap up a little higher on the following bar, but when there aren't any new buyers that come into the market, a narrow range candlestick will show up. A gap down with the following bar will complete the pattern, and it will predict that you will continue to see a decline with really low lows and a downward trend. If you use this option, it means that the prices will continue going down for right now, and you may be able to purchase a stock for a good price.

You can also work with the abandoned baby candlestick strategy. This is another bullish option that you can use, and it will appear at the low of a downtrend, right after there is a series of black candles that print out some new lows. The market will gap even lower on the next bar, but when there aren't any new sellers to help out, it will yield a narrow range Doji candlestick at the opening and closing prints at the same price. Then there will be a bullish gap on the third bar that will help to complete the pattern, and it will predict that the recovery will continue to new highs. This is a good one to work with when you are trying to see if the price is about to go up with the stock you want to work with.

Working with candlesticks can be a great way for you to figure out which way the market will go. They are not completely accurate all of the time, but they can give you a good idea of how the trend will continue in the near future and will give you a way to determine if it is time to get into the market or if you need to wait until a later time. Many people like to work with the candlestick strategies because this allows them to look at the market accurately and make the best predictions on what will happen in the future.

## Other strategies that you can use

So far we have talked about some of the most common strategies that you may choose to work with when it comes to swing trading. These strategies can help you to pick out which charts you should work with to see results. There are a few other strategies that you can use to see success with swing trading including:

- **Use technical analysis and the price action:** These are techniques that most swing traders will use. This kind of analysis will make it easier to figure out which stock or option you should trade and for how long you should hold it.

- **Don't spend all the time with a company:** while most long-term investors will focus on the fundamentals of a stock compared to how well it is doing at a particular moment, this is not something that swing trading will worry about. You may want to pick a few stocks to stick with for your trades because this helps you to learn the history and make better predictions, but you don't need to worry yourself about the particulars of the company. The intrinsic value, who runs the company, who owns the company, and what the company does is not all that important unless it will lead to a big increase in stock value over the next few weeks.

- **Stick with the trends:** many swing traders will choose to look at the trends in the market and then use those to help them develop their own strategy. For example, they would use a bull trend bar when they are working with a bull market, and then they would do a bear trend bar any time they are in a downward market.

- **Work against the trend:** It is more common for a swing trader to work with the current trend of their stock or the market they pick. But there are some who decide to work against the trend, something that is known as fading. For example, when the stock is swinging high, they will choose to work with a bearish position, but when there is a downtrend, they will take a bullish position.

- **Japanese candlesticks:** Some new traders like to work with candlestick charts because they are a bit easier to understand compared to a bar chart. You can use these charts to identify where there is pressure for buying and when there is pressure for selling. You can also use these charts to figure out how intense the pressure is at a particular time. If you can read these charts the proper way, it is easier to know which way the market is going and you can make some smart investing choices.

- **T-Line strategy:** With this strategy, you will go look at your charts and identify where the T-line is located to help you make good trading decisions. If you see that a stock is closing above this line, there is a good probability that the price will keep rising. On the other hand, if the stock ends up closing below this line, it is likely that the stock price will keep falling down. In many investment trades, this strategy will prove successful.

Picking out the right strategy will be one of the most important decisions that you will make when it comes to any investment, but especially when you are dealing with swing trading. It will determine what information you are looking at for the market trends and will ensure that you catch the upward trends at the right time. If you can pick out a good strategy and stick with it for the long-term, you will see success with swing trading.

## Figuring out your risk to reward ratio and your profitability

The profitability of the trades that you work with will be the percentage of trades that you complete that end with a profit. So, if you earn a profit on sixty of your trades and you trade 100 times, your ratio will be sixty percent.

On the other hand, the risk to reward ratio will be the amount that you end up risking compared to the amount that you are working to gain. As a beginner, it is best to pick a risk to reward ratio that is no worse than 1 to 1. This means that if you risk about five percent on the trade, you would try to make five percent on that trade as well.

This ratio is not going to make you a ton of money, but it does help you form a base and will build up confidence as you go. Depending on the chart pattern that you work with, you may change the ratio around a bit, but this will vary based on the strategy that you want to use. As you become more of a professional trader, you can increase your risk to reward ratio so that you can earn more on each trade.

# Chapter 5:

# The Biggest Rules to
# Follow in Swing Trading

Swing trading can take some time to master. It is easier to work with compared to working with day trading, but it is much harder and requires a lot of patience and time commitment compared to working with some of the longer-term investments that you can choose. Despite this extra work, there is the potential for you to make a big profit with limited risk if you follow the right rules. This chapter will take some time to look at some of the rules that you need to see success when it comes to swing trading.

## Align the trade with the market

When you are trying to figure out what trades to do, you always need to take a look at what the market is doing. The market is not going to behave in the manner that you would like, so you need to learn how the market is about to behave and then pick your trades to go with that.

The overall direction the market will take will be measured through the S&P 500. These trends will provide you with some context for making your short-term trades. Remember that short-term trades will be a bit different than you will find with long-term trends and look at how the market will behave in the next few weeks is more important than worrying about how the market will do over the next few years.

However, you also do need to pay some attention to the trends that happen over the long-term with swing trading. These trends will often show up again and again for a particular stock and take a look at them can help to increase your profit potential. Yes, it is important to take a look at the short-term and see what is going on with the market to see if anything is about to change and then trade along with that trend. The more you can look at the charts, both long-term and short-term the more you will be able to make good decisions on your trades.

## Go short weakness and long strength

You should not avoid or fight off the tape once you figure out what the overall trend is. You need to look at the charts to find long trades that will work during periods of bullishness. And then when you are dealing with periods of bearishness, you need to find the right short trades. These trends will help you to get the results that you would like when it comes to successful swing trading.

## Enter at the beginning rather than the end

One mistake that some beginners will make is that they will try and enter the trend near the end of it, rather than catching the trend at the beginning. This will limit some of the money that you can make if you wait too long to enter into a trend. Of course, it is much better to get into the market at some time for the trend, before it goes down because you will be able to make some money, but the earlier you can get into the trend, the more money you can make.

When looking at the charts, it is important to look for early signs of the change. The earlier you can see these new trends, the less risk you will take with swing trading and the bigger the profits you will make. This means that you have to be active. Trends can go quickly and if you are not careful about what is going on in the market, and you are not looking at the market averages, you will end up missing out on some trends and will miss out on some money, or even lose money.

Looking at the overall market averages on your charts will help out with this. When you look at the market averages, you will sometimes see that the stocks have been oversold or overbought. When this has happened, it means that it is likely they will turn around again soon. If the trend looks like it is about to reverse, you can jump in, get the stock for a good price, and sell it over the next few weeks when things start to go back up.

You need to get some of your own indicators in place to figure out when these trends are about to happen. The Volatility Index, the Put/Call Ratio, and the Arms Index are good tools. You will be able to see, through these methods, when the market is testing a major zone of resistance and support, and it can help you to predict what will happen in the future.

On the other hand, looking at moving average crossovers and trendlines will make you fall behind. These are just going to confirm that a trend is happening and by the time you see them and join in on a trade, it may be too late to make any money. These tools can help you determine if you have made a good decision along the way, but if you are relying solely on them, you will miss out.

## Never trade on one technical concept

With swing trading, things will change on a frequent basis. You need to work with trading quickly, picking up one trade and then selling it within a few weeks. You do not get the benefit of staying with the market for a very long time, or you are missing out on the profits you can make. Relying on just one technical concept will lead you to a lot of trouble along the way.

In most cases, the highly profitable trades will occur when you can find at least two (but more is much better) technical tools send you the same message. There are times when several of your tools will show the same indicators, and this means that the stock will rise or fall sharply in the near future. This is great news for you. The more indicators that show the same information, the more likely that the trend is about to occur and that you will make a large profit in the process.

However, there are times when one indicator will show that a trend is about to occur. If you only look at that one indicator, you may find out after entering the trade that it is wrong. You want to have at least a few indicators in place to help you make your decisions. The best opportunities for swing trading will show up in at least a few indicators, and when you can get three or more of these to show up with the same message over a two or three day period, this will increase your profitability.

## Enter the trade with a good plan

There are a lot of different strategies and plans that you can go with. Many of them can be successful when it comes to swing trading, but you do need to pick out a good one and stick with it. One of the worst things that a beginner can do is get started with a strategy, see that it is maybe not doing as well as they had hoped, and then skipping over to a new strategy right in the middle of their trade. This is setting yourself up for failure, and you are more likely to lose money with this method than any other.

It is fine to switch out the types of strategies that you want to use if you find one is not the best for you. But you must make sure that you pick out a strategy and use it for the whole time of your trade. Even if the trade is not going the way that you would like, stick with the strategy. This will limit your risks, and you will learn more from the experience in the long run. If a strategy is not the right one for you, simply switch to a different one the next time.

## Try to work the odds

You are not able to make the market work the way that you would like. The market will behave however it would like. There are a lot of different people who are in the market, and the swing trading will only take place over a few days. You need to learn how to work with the market, rather than trying to influence it.

It is never a good idea to risk a dollar just so you can make a dime. You have to pick out smart trades, trades that will lower your risk as much as possible while making your high profits. There will be some trades that may promise a lot of money if you try them, but the risk is so high that you are likely to lose all of your investment plus more without making anything.

The best trades that you can do are ones that will provide you with a strong profit if you make the right types of decisions, but where you can limit your losses as much as possible if you are wrong. The profits may not be as big as some of the trades that you can make, but it ensures that you will not lose out on all your investment either.

## Learn to control the emotions a little bit

The most important thing that you can do when you get into swing trading is learning how to keep your emotions out of the game. This is important no matter which investment you choose, but it is especially important when you are working with some of these short-term investments. Once your emotions get into the mix, it is a lot harder to make smart decisions and smart trades that will lead to profits.

If you let your emotions get into the mix, you are likely to make poor trading decisions. You will make decisions that will lead you to lose money. You will stay in the market too long, hoping to earn more money, or hoping that you can recover some of your losses. Basically, when you start letting the emotions get into the mix, you are risking your money, and you will end up losing out on all your hard work.

For those who are not able to think through their decisions critically, who are not able to keep their emotions out of the trades that they will do, it is much better to just stay out of the market completely. Swing trading needs some fast decision making and the help of a lot of research. If you are not able to do this without all the emotions, you will fail in the long run.

## Do your trading with a consistent group of stocks

When you first get started with day trading, it is pretty easy to jump around between stocks. You may find on that looks good and then want to jump to another once the trade is all done. There is nothing wrong with following the action, but it is always best to have your core stocks that you track on a regular basis and learn how they work.

Having a few regular stocks is a great way to see regular success with swing trading. These regular stocks will allow you to learn about the market better and can save a lot of time researching. You will have time to learn how the stocks work and understand how they have performed in the past and are likely to perform in the future. It takes some of the work out of it all when you can stick with a few core stocks over the long term.

Of course, there is nothing wrong going with a new stock on occasion if you see some big trends that are coming up. This can be a great way to increase your profit, especially if you have been in the market for some time. But chasing after those new stocks can take up a lot of work. Learn as much about your core stocks as possible, and you will save a lot of work, reduce your risk, and increase your profits.

Everyone will spend time working with different methods and strategies when it comes to swing trading. And even with different methods, it is possible to see many people make a profit. If you follow some of these rules and learn how to pick the right strategy, you will see some great results when it comes to swing trading.

# Chapter 6:

# The Top Mistakes
# That Beginners Make

As a beginner, there are a lot of things that you need to learn to do well with swing trading. Learning all the strategies, learning how to read the charts, and making smart decisions when it comes to picking out stocks to work with can be a challenge. As you are getting used to the whole process, it can take some time and effort, and you are likely to make some mistakes along the way.

These mistakes are pretty normal when you are a beginner, but no beginner wants to deal with them. They want to be able to make as much money as possible, without losing a lot of money as they start to learn how things work. This chapter focuses on some of the top mistakes that a lot of beginners make and some of the things that you can do to avoid these common mistakes.

## Let the emotions get in the way

One mistake that almost all beginners will make is that they let their emotions get in the way of their decision making. They see that they are about to lose out on a trade or they see that the profits will keep reaching a higher value, and they want to stay in the market longer, despite what all their research and their strategy told them before. This will end up disastrous and is one of the leading reasons that beginners lose so much money and end up having to stop at day trading.

You need to learn how to keep the emotions out of the game. If you are a highly emotional person, swing trading is not going to be the best option for you to try out because things can change in an instant. The good news is that there are a few techniques that you can use to help keep the emotions out of the game so you can reduce your risk and increase your chances of profit.

First, make sure that you use stop points and that you stick with them. These stop points will ensure that you enter and exit the trade at the right times to either limit your losses or to help limit the risk that you have while gaining a profit.

They aren't always full proof, but if you stick with them, you are less likely to have issues later on. Picking a good strategy, asking for advice, and really doing your research before you begin are all good ways to ensure you can keep the emotions out of your trading.

## Forget to use stop points

The stop points will be so important when you start out as a swing trader. These points will tell you when to get out of the market, whether the market is going up or down and can reduce your risk. You need to have a stop loss point, which is the point you will get out of the market if you lose so much money, and you need a stop profit point, which is where you will get out of the market once you earn a certain profit.

Both of these are important to ensure you cut down on your risk and that you make as much money as possible in the process. For the stop loss point, you are figuring out how much money you are comfortable with losing in the market. Once the market goes down to this point, you need to get out. It is highly likely that the market will keep going down and if you don't get out at your stop loss point, you will potentially lose a lot of money in the process. This takes the emotions out of the game. You simply see that the stop point was reached and cut your losses until the next trade.

You also need to have a stop point for the profits that you want to earn. This may seem silly because you want to earn as much profit as you possibly can with each trade. But emotions can come into play here again too. Without the stop point, you may end up staying in the market too long, and make some costly mistakes. The market can turn around just as quickly as it went up, and if you are still in the market, you may lose all your earnings instead of gaining anything.

For this stop point, figure out what you can realistically make on the trade. Where do you think the market for your stock will go over the next few days based on the trend that you are setting? Put the stop point there and then as soon as the market reaches that point, you will take your earnings and withdraw from the market.

## Putting in more money than you can afford to lose

With any investment that you work with, you need to be careful about the losses that you are dealing with. If you take on too much risk, you will end up losing all your money and never getting a chance to give it another try. Coming up with a good risk to reward ratio will help to limit your losses, but you also must make sure that you never put in more than you are willing to lose.

A good place to start is to put some savings behind for your swing trades. Never use money that you would need for rent, food, and other necessities. The second you do this, you bring the emotions into the game, and you are more likely to lose it all. Starting a savings account right now with the money you can use for swing trading allows you to have a little cushion without having to eat up all the money you need for other things.

When you are using the extra money, rather than money that you really need elsewhere, you are ensuring that you will spend it wisely. You won't stay in a trade too long in the hopes of recovering that money. No one wants to lose money along the way when they are trading, but it is much easier to cut your losses when it was just a little savings rather than if that money was your rent payment for the month.

## Not understanding your strategy

If you do not understand the strategy that you are using, it can be impossible for you to get results when you get started with swing trading. Your strategy will outline exactly how you will behave in each trade situation. It will tell you how to look at the charts, how to pick out the stocks, when to enter the market, and when to exit the market. Each strategy has the potential to be successful, but you need to understand the strategy and use it properly.

When you get started in swing trading, it is always best to start with a simple strategy. Yes, there are some more complex ones that may sound fun, but since you are already learning about the market and how it works, why add in more complications with a hard strategy. There are a lot of great strategies that are simple, and some even designed for the beginner, that will make you just as much money as the more complex strategies, without all the work.

Picking a strategy is really important when it comes to doing well in swing trading. Before you pick out one, make sure to read through them all and fully understand what you will need to do to make it successful. You want one that is effective and easy to follow, as well as one that you will not want to switch out of in the middle of the trade. There is nothing wrong with trying out different strategies to see which one you like the best in between your trades, but if you switch strategies while in the same trade, you are setting yourself up for failure.

## Not having the right tools

As a trader, you need to have some of your own tools in place if you would like to get started with swing trading. This can be a very difficult method when it comes to investing, and without the right tools, you will miss out on some important information that can help you see trends and make smart decisions along the way.

The first place to go for some tools is to talk to your broker. Often the broker will have a variety of unique tools that they can give to you as part of their fees. If you don't know how to use some of these tools, make sure to ask questions and learn how to make it all work or you will miss out.

You can also bring in some of your own tools to the game as well. Find charts about the market, look online, and ask questions. Remember, the best way to notice a trend is when the same information starts to show up on more than one chart or tool so always strive to have as many of these tools available as possible.

## Following others rather than learning your own way

When you first get started, it can be tempting to find a mentor or a group and then just follow along exactly with what they do each time. This is really tempting if you see that they are making a lot of money and you want to join and make that money as well. But in the long run, no one knows the trading style that you like, and there are times when even an advanced mentor will get things wrong.

Instead of following along blindly with what someone else tells you, it is better to learn your own way. There is nothing wrong with talking to a mentor and others who have been in the market for some time, but you need to learn your own methods, your own strategies, and how you want to behave in the market. This will help you to stay on track with your trades and will ensure that you don't get misled by others who may not have your best interests at heart.

## Not cutting your losses

Even the best swing traders will make mistakes at times. They will misread the market, they will try out a new strategy that doesn't work for them, or the market just doesn't behave in the manner that they had hoped. And when this happens, the trader will lose out on their money. As a beginner, it is more likely that you will earn a loss at some point. The important thing is to learn how to cut your losses, rather than staying too long in the market.

Some beginners will see that they are losing money on one of their trades and so they will try to regain that money. Even with the market going down, and no signs of reversal, they will stay in the market and hope that things will reverse. This is dangerous because it results in you staying in the market way too long and you will lose out on way too much money in the process.

Instead of sticking with a market that is not working in your favor, it is much better to learn how to cut your losses. Pick out an amount that you are comfortable with losing if the market does not go the way that you would like, put a stop point there, and then withdraw from the market as soon as you reach that point. This will help you to limit your losses and can give you more opportunities to try another trade in the future.

## Using vengeance trading

Vengeance trading is one of the worst things you can do as a new trader. It forces you to make unsafe trading decisions in the hopes of earning some of your money back after a loss. Unfortunately, since you are only thinking about earning your money back, and not about the decisions that will help you to limit your risks as a trader, you will end up losing a lot of money in the process.

It can be hard if you lose a lot of money on one of your trades. Everyone who gets into swing trading drams about making a lot of money and doing well with this investment. However, as a beginner, there will be times when you make mistakes or the market doesn't behave the way that you would like and you will lose some money in the process.

If you lose money and then start becoming desperate to make that money back right away, you have let your emotions get in the way. While it is normal to want to lose as little as possible with swing trading, you need to focus on picking a good strategy and learning how to read the market next time, rather than worrying about how to earn your money back. If you make smart decisions with swing trading, you will earn all the money back and more, but if you get stuck in vengeance trading, you will end up losing all your money in the process.

As a beginner, there is a lot to learn when it comes to swing trading. Swing trading can take some time and energy, and it is not as easy as you may think when you first get started. But if you learn how to get rid of some of these mistakes and you pick a good strategy to help you out, you are sure to see some great results in no time.

# Conclusion

Thank you for making it through to the end of this book, let's hope it was informative and able to provide you with all of the tools you need to achieve your goals whatever they may be.

The next step is to decide whether swing trading is the right option for you to go with. There are a lot of different investment options that you can choose to go with, and some will be easier than swing trading. On the other hand, not all of them will provide you with the high potential profit in a short amount of time as you can get with swing trading.

This guidebook provided you with the information that you need to get started with swing trading. Swing trading is hard to get started with and will require you to spend some time looking at charts and understanding the best steps that you can take to be successful with this trading method. We will look at some of the strategies that work well with swing trading, the rules that you need to follow, some of the benefits of swing trading, and so much more.

Swing trading is a fantastic way to make money in no time when it comes to the stock market. It gives you some more time to make decisions, but you can still make money in a short amount of time from between a day to a few weeks. Make sure to check out this guidebook when you are ready to get started with swing trading.

Finally, if you found this book useful in any way, a review on Amazon is always appreciated!

# Description

There are many different types of investing that you can work with. You can work with the stock market, choose to save for your retirement, start a business, and even work in real estate. But if you would like to make a good amount of profit in a short amount of time, then it may be time to consider swing trading.

This guidebook discusses thing you need to know about swing trading and how it is different from some of the other stock market trading options that you can go with. Some of the topics that we will discuss about swing trading includes:

- What swing trading is
- The benefits of swing trading
- How to get started swing trading
- Top strategies for success with swing trading
- The biggest rules to follow in swing trading
- The top mistakes that beginners make

When you are ready to get started with swing trading and making a good profit within a week or less, make sure to read through this guidebook and learn everything that you need to get started.